Space
and Sky

By
Virginie Loubier

Illustrated by
Robert Barborini
Audrey Brien
Hélène Convert
Christian Guibbaud
Cristian Turdera

Twirl

Contents

Index 77

The "Let's Review!" pages at the end of each section help reinforce learning.

Index Quickly find the word you're looking for with the index at the end of the book.

Look for the colored boxes in the bottom right-hand corners. You will find references to related subjects in other parts of the book.

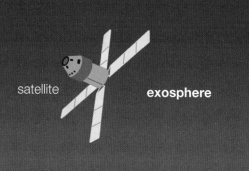

satellite

exosphere

thermosphere

mesosphere

stratosphere

troposphere

rain

cloud

Why
is the sky blue
?

When the Sun is up, the sky is blue, no matter where you are in the world.

Sunlight is made up of many colors. When this light reaches our atmosphere, molecules in the air scatter blue light more than any other color.

The blue light gets separated from the other colors, so we see more of that color in the sky!

Telescopes **44**
High above Earth **46**

The Water Cycle

All the water in the world travels from lakes, rivers, oceans, and other bodies of water to the atmosphere and back to Earth. This process has taken place for billions of years!

mountain

Sun

condensation
(Water vapor changes back to liquid and gathers as clouds.)

precipitation
(Water falls back to Earth as rain, snow, or ice.)

surface runoff

stream

evaporation
(Water changes from liquid to vapor.)

estuary

back to the sea

sea

river

source

infiltration

groundwater

Weather

Meteorologists study the atmosphere to observe, research, and forecast the weather.

thermometer, to measure temperature

gathering data

meteorologist

You may have noticed that rainbows often appear when it's sunny and raining at the same time.

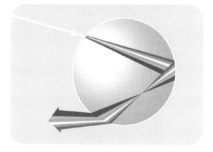

As the light enters each raindrop, it bends and is reflected off the inside of the droplet. When it leaves the droplet, the light separates into various colors.

wind

rain

clouds

storm

fog

sunshine

snow

weather reporter

There are as many colors as there are days of the week: red, orange, yellow, green, blue, indigo, and violet.

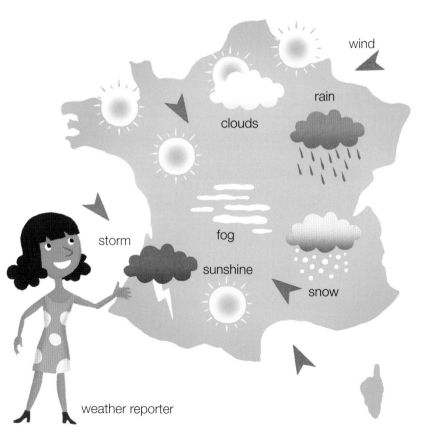

Seasons **15**

Earth **28**

🚲 Revolving and Rotating

Earth revolves around the Sun, but it also spins on its own axis, at about 1,000 miles (1,600 kilometers) per hour.

The **Moon** takes about 27 days to both completely rotate on its own axis and revolve around Earth.

Galileo, a scientist who first used the telescope for astronomy

GALILEO

Earth completes a rotation on its own axis in 24 hours (one day).

What
did people once believe about the Sun **?**

Earth takes 365 days (one year) to revolve around the **Sun**.

satellite

People used to believe that Earth was the center of the universe, and that the Sun and other planets revolved around it.

The Sun takes about 27 days to rotate on its own axis and 230 million years to revolve around the center of our galaxy. But it does not revolve around Earth.

In the early 1500s, scientist Nicolaus Copernicus proposed that Earth and other planets move around the Sun. It took almost 100 years before people believed him.

Day and Night

On the side of Earth that is facing the Sun, it is day. On the other side, it is night.

morning

midday

evening

night

flashlight

day

globe

learning about
Earth's rotation

Seasons

Earth's axis is slightly tilted. That is why we have seasons. The part of Earth that directly faces the Sun gets the most heat.

Earth

spring

summer

Sun

winter

autumn

In the evening, you can see the Sun disappear over the horizon little by little, as if it were going to bed when night falls.

This is not because the Sun has moved, but rather that Earth is rotating on its own axis.

In the daytime, you can see the Sun from where you are. It takes 24 hours, or one day and one night, for Earth to turn completely around.

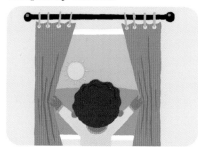

Revolving and Rotating **12**
Eclipses **18**

Phases of the Moon

The Moon does not change its shape, but it does look different sometimes, depending on where it is in relation to Earth and the Sun.

waxing crescent

first quarter

third quarter

waning crescent

What is the Moon **?**

full moon

new moon

The Moon shines light on Earth at night, but it is not a star.

It does not give off light. The Moon's surface actually reflects the light of the Sun, the same way a mirror can reflect light.

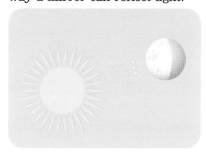

The Moon is called a natural satellite because it revolves around Earth.

Eclipses

A solar eclipse occurs when the Moon passes in front of the Sun. A lunar eclipse occurs when Earth passes between the Moon and the Sun.

solar eclipse

Sun

total eclipse

The Moon gradually blocks the Sun's light.

The Sun gradually reappears as the Moon moves away.

solar eclipse glasses, to protect your eyes

lunar eclipse

partial eclipse

total eclipse

Earth's shadow

Moon

Earth blocks the Sun's light from reaching the Moon.

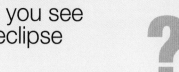

Total solar eclipses happen about once every 18 months. They usually last only a few minutes.

Lunar eclipses occur at least once or twice a year. You may see them, depending on where you live.

Find out when the next total solar eclipse or lunar eclipse will take place. Don't forget to write it on the calendar!

Let's Review!

Can you name the missing layers of the atmosphere?

exosphere ·······················

? ·······················

mesosphere ·······················

? ·······················

? ·······················

What kind of weather does each picture show?

Point to each phase of the Moon in the correct order. Can you name them?

What is happening in this picture?
What are the people wearing
over their eyes?

The Solar System

Our Cosmic Neighborhood

Our solar system is made up of a star—the Sun—eight planets, and millions of smaller bodies, asteroids, comets, and dwarf planets.

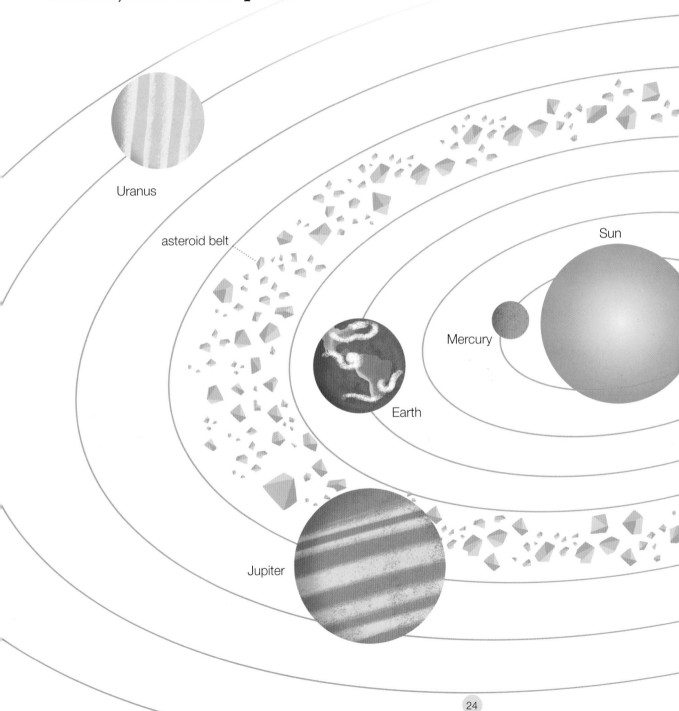

Uranus

asteroid belt

Sun

Mercury

Earth

Jupiter

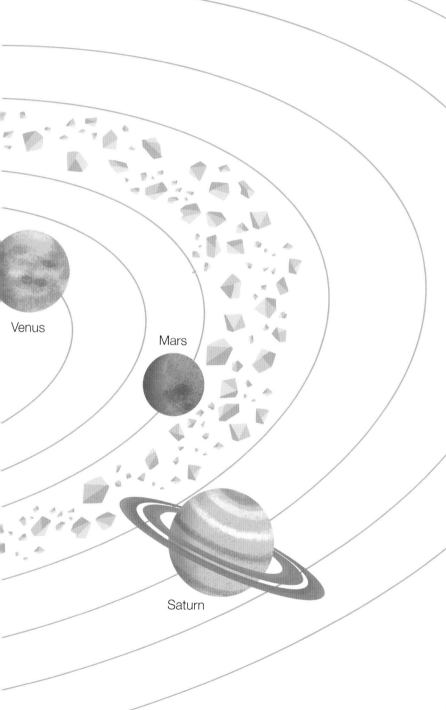

Neptune

Venus

Mars

Saturn

You might have read stories that take place on planets outside our solar system.

They are called exoplanets, and astronomers have discovered thousands of them! We don't yet know which ones support life.

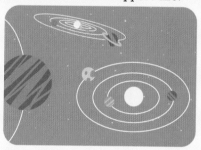

Most exoplanets orbit stars, but some, called rogue planets, float freely. No one knows what these planets look like—or who lives there. What do you think?

The Sun

Earth revolves around the Sun, a star that is more than one hundred times larger than our planet. Without the heat from the Sun, there would not be life on Earth.

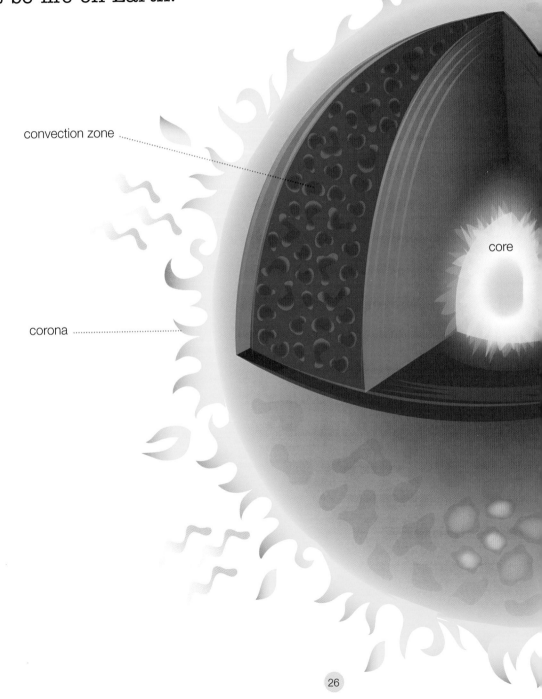

light

convection zone

core

corona

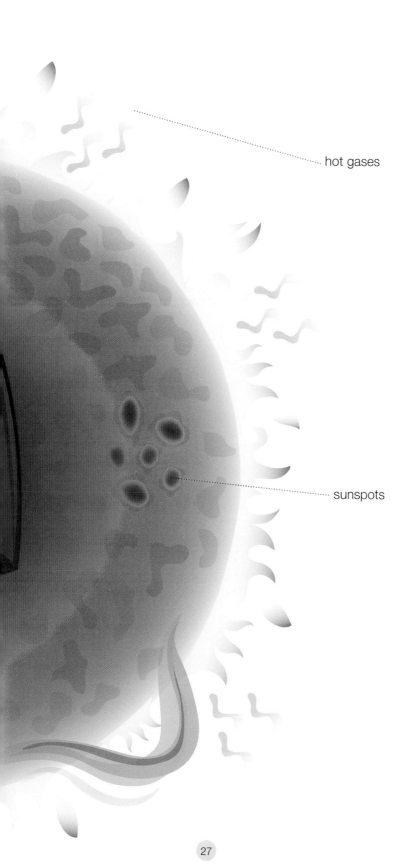

hot gases

sunspots

Why
does the
Sun shine

?

The Sun is an enormous ball of extremely hot gas. The temperature in its core is about 27 million degrees Fahrenheit (15 million degrees Celsius).

This heat is the reason why the Sun "shines," producing the sunlight necessary to light up our days and the warmth to support life on Earth.

Some homes have solar panels, which gather sunlight and turn it into electrical energy.

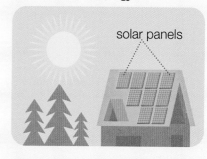

solar panels

Revolving and Rotating **12**

Eclipses **18**

Earth

Earth is the third-closest planet to the Sun. It is the only known planet that has an atmosphere of oxygen and bodies of water, both of which are necessary to support life.

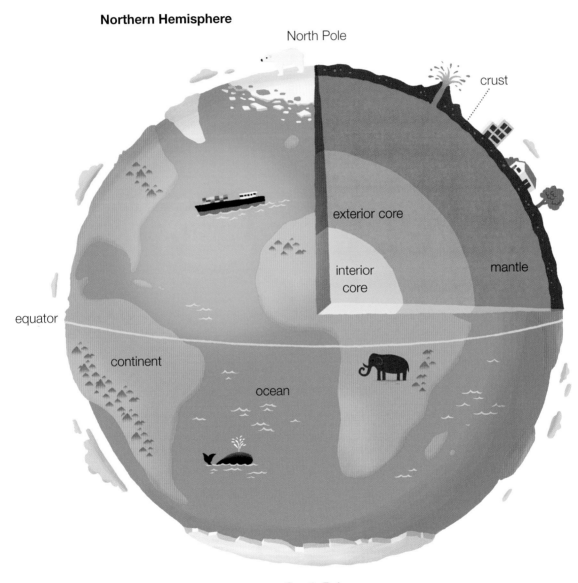

Northern Hemisphere

North Pole

crust

exterior core

interior core

mantle

equator

continent

ocean

South Pole

Southern Hemisphere

🌑 The Moon

The Moon is our planet's only natural satellite. It is about 240,000 miles (385,000 kilometers) away from Earth. Its surface is covered with dark and light areas of craters and mountains.

Craters are formed when asteroids and comets hit the surface.

visible side of the Moon

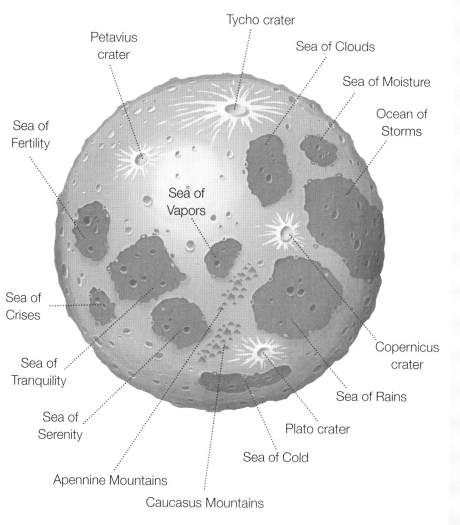

- Petavius crater
- Tycho crater
- Sea of Clouds
- Sea of Moisture
- Ocean of Storms
- Sea of Fertility
- Sea of Vapors
- Sea of Crises
- Sea of Tranquility
- Copernicus crater
- Sea of Serenity
- Sea of Rains
- Plato crater
- Apennine Mountains
- Sea of Cold
- Caucasus Mountains

The seas, which show up as dark patches, are actually large areas of hardened lava.

29

Earth is a unique planet. It is the only one in our solar system that supports life for plants, animals, and humans.

Life exists on Earth because its atmosphere contains oxygen, and there is plenty of water.

Earth is also a comfortable distance away from the Sun, so we have the perfect amount of heat and light.

High above Earth **46**
The First Step on the Moon **62**

Types of Planets

In our solar system, there are three types of planets: terrestrial ones with rocky surfaces, gas giants, and ice giants.

ice giants

Uranus
the sideways planet

Neptune
the planet farthest from the Sun

gas giants

Jupiter
the biggest planet

rings

Saturn
the ringed planet

terrestrial planets

Venus
the hottest planet

Mercury
the smallest planet

Mars
the red planet

Earth
the blue planet

What
life-forms exist beyond Earth

?

No one knows if there are extraterrestrials, or beings from other planets. There are books and movies that show what some people think they might look like.

Scientists send space probes to other planets to look for signs of life beyond Earth.

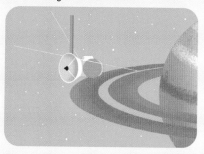

At this time, they believe that the life-forms they might find would be very small organisms, such as bacteria.

The Universe

The universe seems almost infinite. It contains everything that exists: stars, planets, living things, light, galaxies, and even time.

stars

galaxies

gas cloud

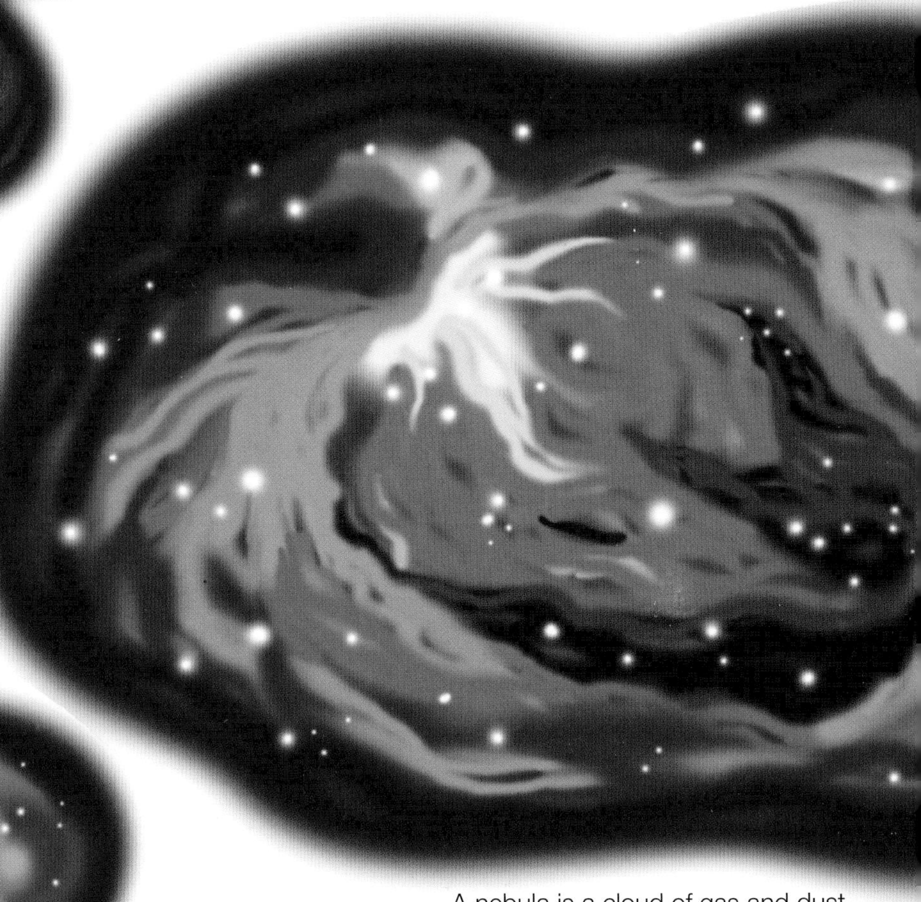

A nebula is a cloud of gas and dust. Some nebulae are areas where new stars form.

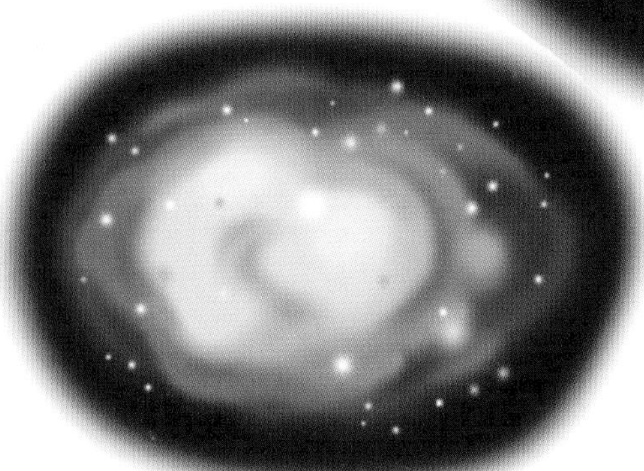

solar system

dust ring

black hole

dark matter

Astronomers, scientists who study space, believe that the universe was formed about 14 billion years ago when a small fireball exploded.

This idea is known as the big bang theory. After that explosion, the universe started expanding—just as a balloon does when you blow air into it.

What we know of the universe right now is just a very small part of it. There is much more that has yet to be discovered.

The Milky Way **42**

Telescopes **44**

Let's Review!

What are the missing names of these planets? Can you place them in order, starting from the one closest to the Sun to the one farthest away?

Jupiter

Uranus

Can you find a sea, a crater, and mountains on the Moon's surface?

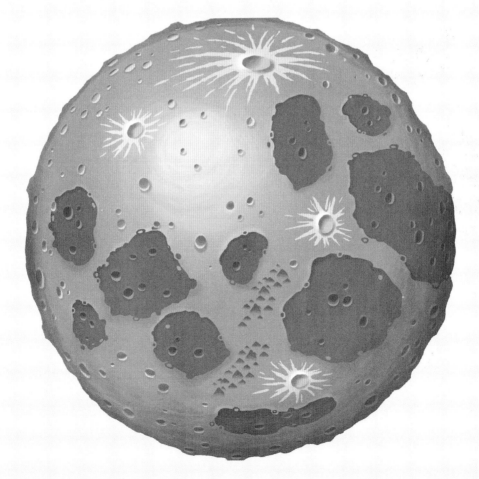

Name the planets that are terrestrial, gas giants, and ice giants.

Jupiter

Mars

Neptune

Uranus

Earth

Saturn

Venus

Mercury

Earth is the only planet in our solar system where human beings can live. Can you explain why?

Studying the Universe

The Stars

Stars are huge balls of gas that light up the night sky. Groups of stars that make patterns or shapes are called constellations.

constellations

Draco

Ursa Major

Ursa Minor

Leo Minor

Polaris or North Star

observing the stars

binoculars

Camelopardalis

sky chart

telescope

shooting star

Cygnus

Cepheus

Lacerta

Cassiopeia

Andromeda

What
is a shooting star ?

A shooting star is not a star. It's a small piece of rock or dust called a meteoroid that enters Earth's atmosphere.

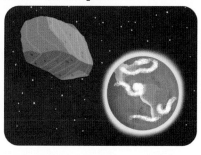

The light you see is the meteoroid burning up as it moves very quickly through our sky.

You don't need special equipment to look at shooting stars—just your eyes!

Telescopes **44**
High above Earth **46**

Galaxies

A galaxy includes stars, gases, dust, and planets. There are billions of galaxies in the universe, and they don't all have the same shape.

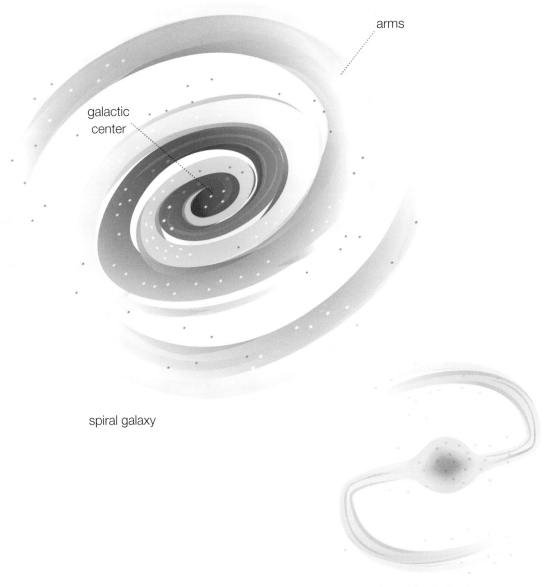

arms

galactic center

spiral galaxy

barred spiral galaxy

elliptical galaxy

irregular galaxy

lenticular galaxy

The universe is constantly expanding, and new galaxies can change and merge over time.

Astronomers know about only a small part of the universe—the "observable" universe. They have estimated that there are 200 billion galaxies.

Research has also shown that there are many more galaxies than that. Scientists are working to build new telescopes that can provide clearer information.

The Milky Way

Our solar system is located in a galaxy called the Milky Way.

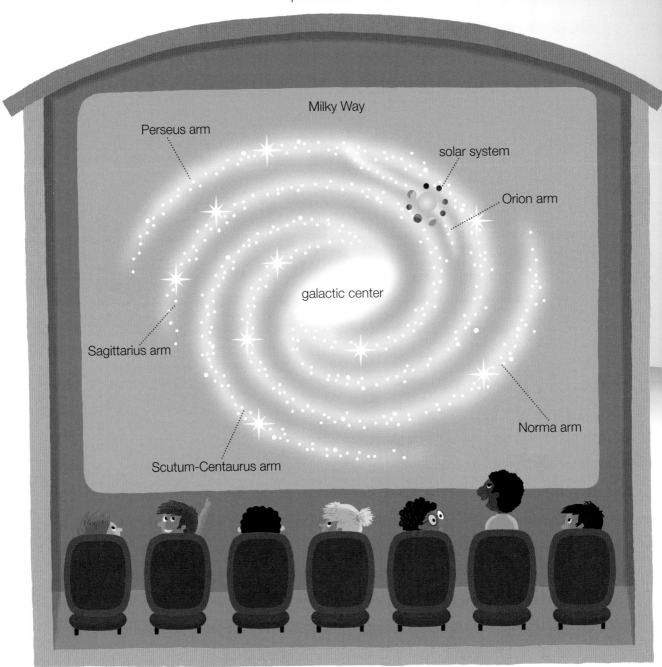

panoramic screen

Milky Way

Perseus arm

solar system

Orion arm

galactic center

Sagittarius arm

Norma arm

Scutum-Centaurus arm

the interstellar medium, a mix of gases and dust

The Milky Way may have 200 billion to 400 billion stars, possibly more!

How

can you see the Milky Way ?

The bright lights in cities and towns prevent many of us from getting a good look at the Milky Way.

The brightest part of the Milky Way is most visible between June and August. It's best seen on nights when it's really dark and there are few clouds.

There are many "dark sky parks" around the world where you can see the Milky Way more easily.

Telescopes

To get images of space, distant planets, or other galaxies, astronomers use powerful telescopes.

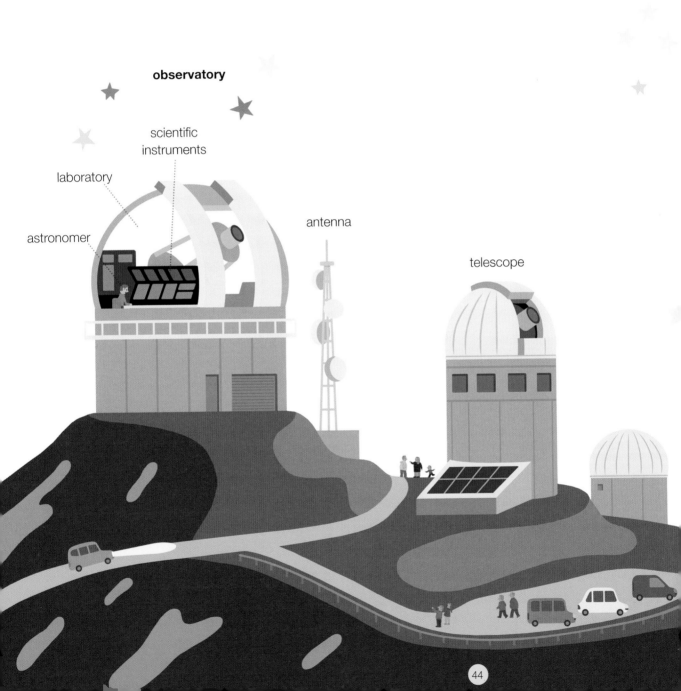

observatory

scientific instruments

laboratory

astronomer

antenna

telescope

Hubble Space Telescope

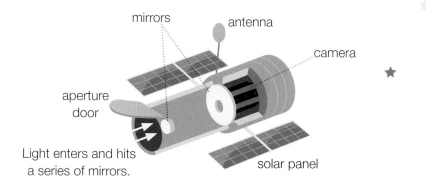

mirrors

antenna

camera

aperture door

Light enters and hits a series of mirrors.

solar panel

The many lights in your neighborhood might make it hard to spot stars in the sky at night.

Scientists use very advanced optical telescopes that are often built in observatories high in the mountains, in areas where skies are clear and the air is dry.

Radio telescopes use dishes to collect radio waves from objects in space and send them to a computer. This information is studied by astronomers.

radio telescope

ladder

🌀 High above Earth

Observing Earth from the sky helps us understand our planet better.

aurora, or polar lights

atmosphere

clouds

North America

Atlantic Ocean

cyclone

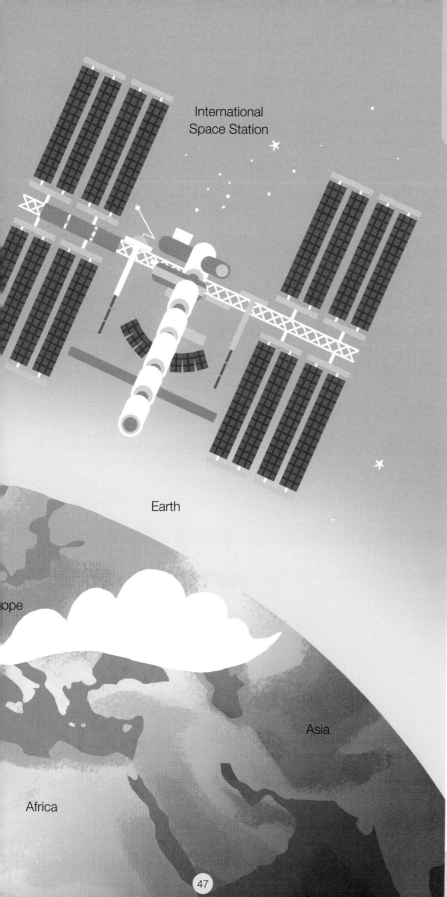

International
Space Station

Earth

ope

Africa

Asia

Why
is Earth called
the blue planet
?

When you see a picture of Earth taken from space, you'll notice a lot of blue areas. These are oceans, seas, rivers, lakes, and other bodies of water.

Water, our most important resource, makes up about 70 percent of Earth's surface. Most of Earth's water is in the oceans. It is salt water.

Fresh water can be found in lakes, ponds, rivers, and glaciers. This is the kind of water we drink.

Earth **28**
The International Space Station **64**

🚀 Rocket

Travel to space is possible because of the invention of rockets, which have engines that are much more powerful than those in airplanes.

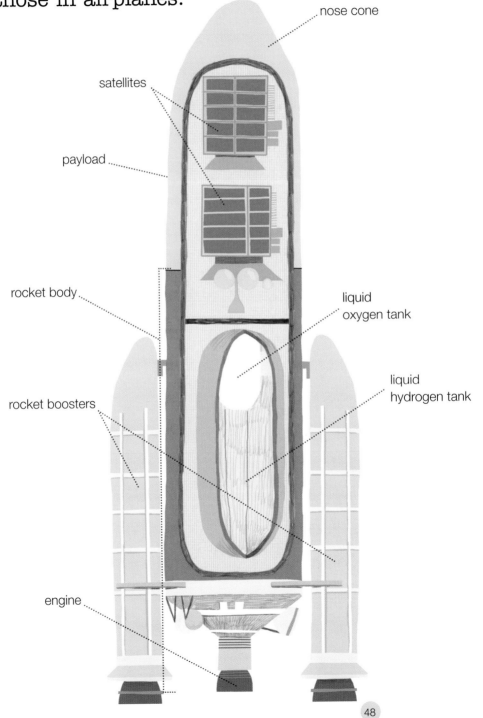

nose cone

satellites

payload

rocket body

liquid oxygen tank

rocket boosters

liquid hydrogen tank

engine

⬛ The Flight

At liftoff, the rocket launches into space. Its parts gradually separate from each other. Finally, the satellite is released.

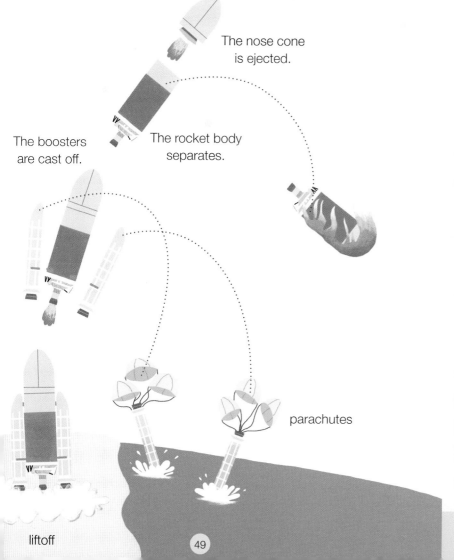

The satellite begins its planned orbit.

The nose cone is ejected.

The boosters are cast off.

The rocket body separates.

parachutes

Rockets are used to carry astronauts, cargo, and other equipment into outer space.

They are also used to launch satellites, which orbit Earth in the thermosphere.

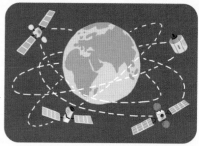

Radio and TV satellites allow us to enjoy our favorite movies, music, games, and TV shows in our homes.

liftoff

From Past to Present **56**
The Launch Site **60**

Satellites

Satellites play an important role in modern communication, help scientists study Earth and space, and track weather patterns.

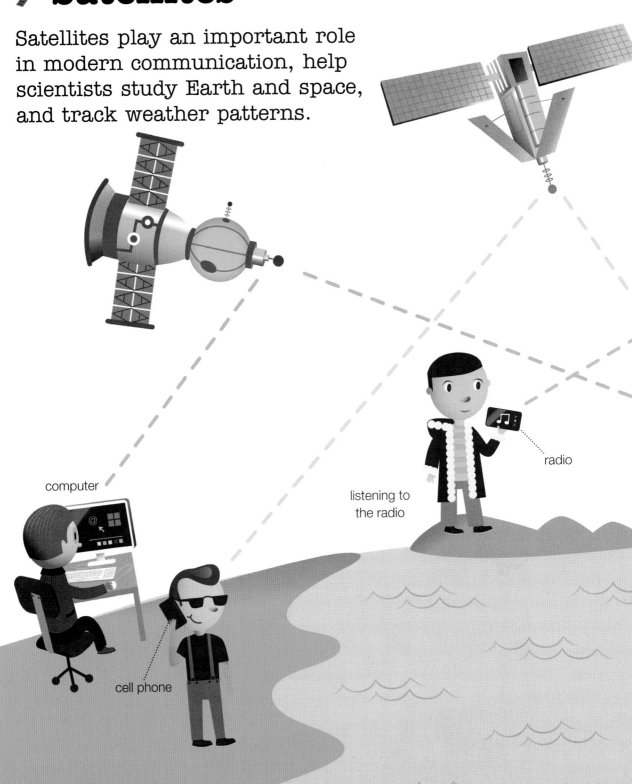

computer

radio

listening to the radio

cell phone

What
happens to
old satellites

?

satellite

using the internet

radio host

making an
international call

Sometimes you might see a light in the sky and think it's a star or an airplane. It may actually be a satellite.

There are thousands of satellites out in space. Some of them no longer function and become space debris, or space junk.

Discarding trash in space is not as easy as getting rid of trash on Earth. Some space junk can be sent farther out into space.

Let's Review!

Use your finger to trace a line between a constellation and its name.

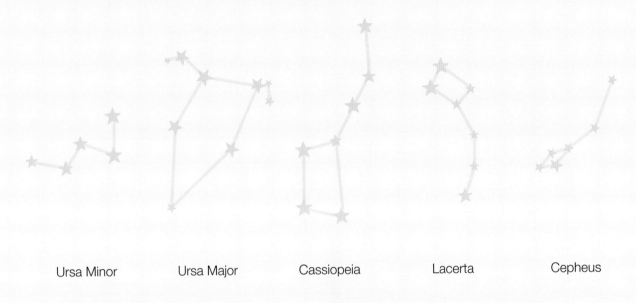

Ursa Minor   Ursa Major   Cassiopeia   Lacerta   Cepheus

Match each telescope with its shadow.
Where might you find these telescopes?

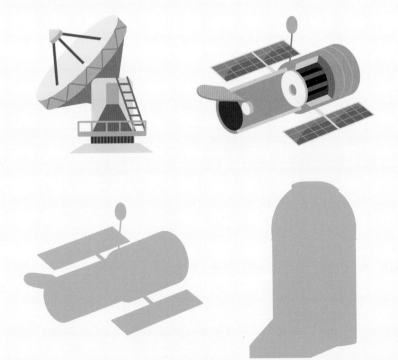

This rocket is launching a satellite. Can you put the steps in order?

Which continents do you see in this picture?
How do views of Earth from space help scientists?

Galaxies can have very different shapes.
Do you have a favorite shape?
Which shape is our galaxy?

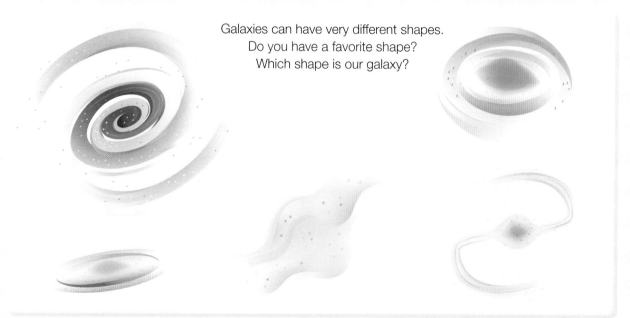

Exploring Space

From Past to Present

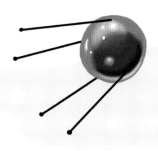

1957, Sputnik 1:
first satellite in space

1957, Sputnik 2:
Laika the dog, first living
thing in space

1961, Vostok 1 mission:
Yuri Gagarin, first human
in space

1986, Mir: Assembly
of the first "permanent"
space station begins.

1981, Columbia space shuttle:
launch of the first reusable
spacecraft

1979, Ariane: launch of
the first European rocket

1986, Challenger space shuttle:
in-flight explosion with seven
astronauts on board

1990: launch of the
Hubble Space
Telescope

1997, Mars Pathfinder
mission: exploration
of Mars with the robot Rocky

1998: launch of the fir
module of the Internatic
Space Station (ISS)

1965, Voskhod 2 mission: Alexei Leonov, first human to perform a spacewalk

1969, Apollo 11 mission: Neil Armstrong, first human to step foot on the Moon

1976, Viking 1 and Viking 2 probes: first explorations of Mars

1971, Mars 3 probe: first successful landing on Mars

2012: Curiosity rover is sent to Mars.

Present day: International crews continue to work on board the ISS.

You might have met an astronaut at your school or at a special event.

Hundreds of astronauts have traveled to space. Did you know that Russian astronauts are called cosmonauts? Astronauts from China are taikonauts.

Astronauts from all over the world live and work together on board the International Space Station for months at a time.

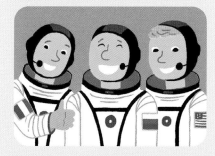

Astronaut Training

Astronauts need to have degrees in the sciences or math, be able to pilot a plane, and be mentally and physically fit.

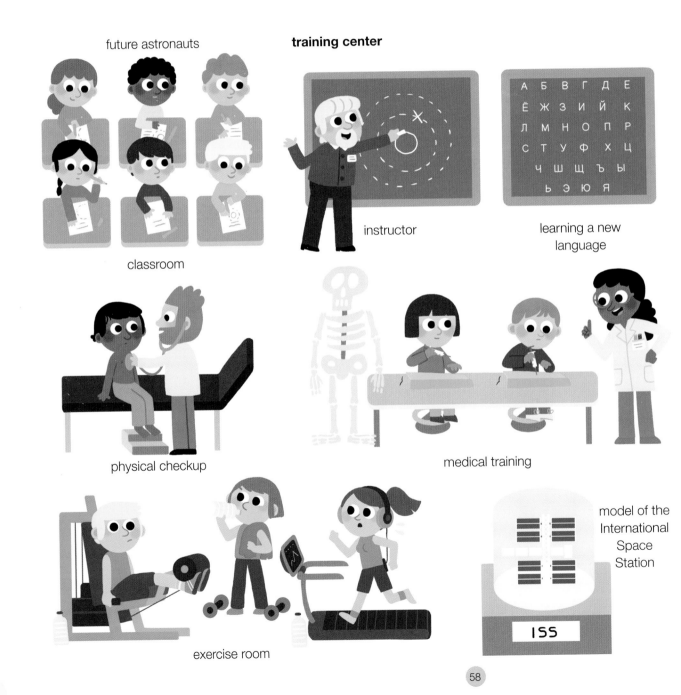

future astronauts

training center

instructor

learning a new language

classroom

physical checkup

medical training

exercise room

model of the International Space Station

ISS

simulators

zero-gravity aircraft

experiencing weightlessness

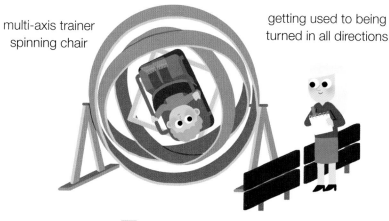

multi-axis trainer spinning chair

getting used to being turned in all directions

centrifuge

preparing astronauts for the different forces that push on them during liftoff

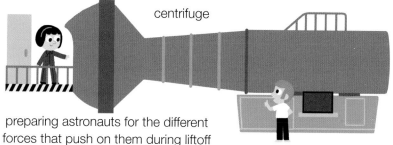

going underwater to practice for a spacewalk

diver

spacesuit

What is a spacesuit ?

In movies, superheroes fly through space without special equipment. Unfortunately, human beings cannot do this in real life.

Astronauts wear spacesuits to protect themselves from the extreme conditions of space. The special suits also supply them with oxygen and water.

The visor on the helmet is coated with a thin layer of gold, which protects astronauts from the Sun's very bright rays.

The Launch Site

Launch sites are located in remote areas and often near an ocean so rockets can launch and travel safely, away from people and over open water.

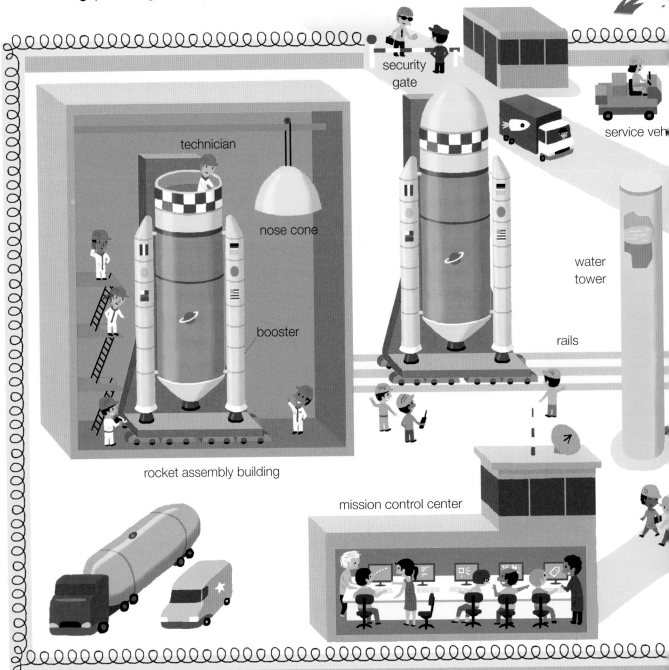

security gate

service veh

technician

nose cone

booster

water tower

rails

rocket assembly building

mission control center

ocean

Have you ever wished you could take a vacation in space? It is a fun idea, but building rockets and training people to go into space takes a lot of time and money.

For now, most travel is limited to scientists who do research and conduct experiments in space. This way, we will know more about our universe.

There are companies that are working to make space travel a regular activity. Perhaps we will be able to go to space for fun one day!

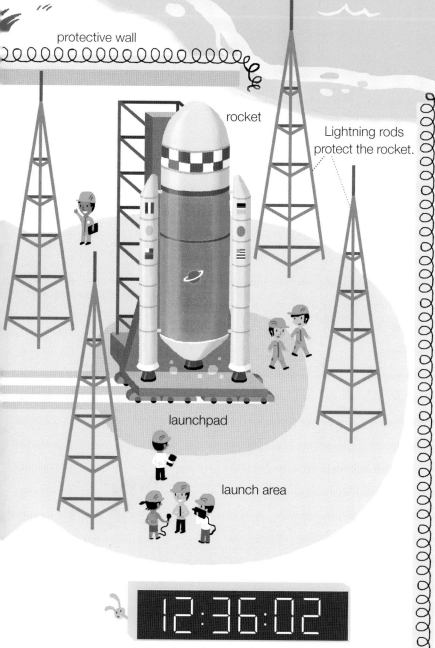

protective wall

rocket

Lightning rods protect the rocket.

launchpad

launch area

12:36:02

launch countdown clock

The First Step on the Moon

In 1969, the Apollo 11 mission carried humans to the surface of the Moon for the very first time.

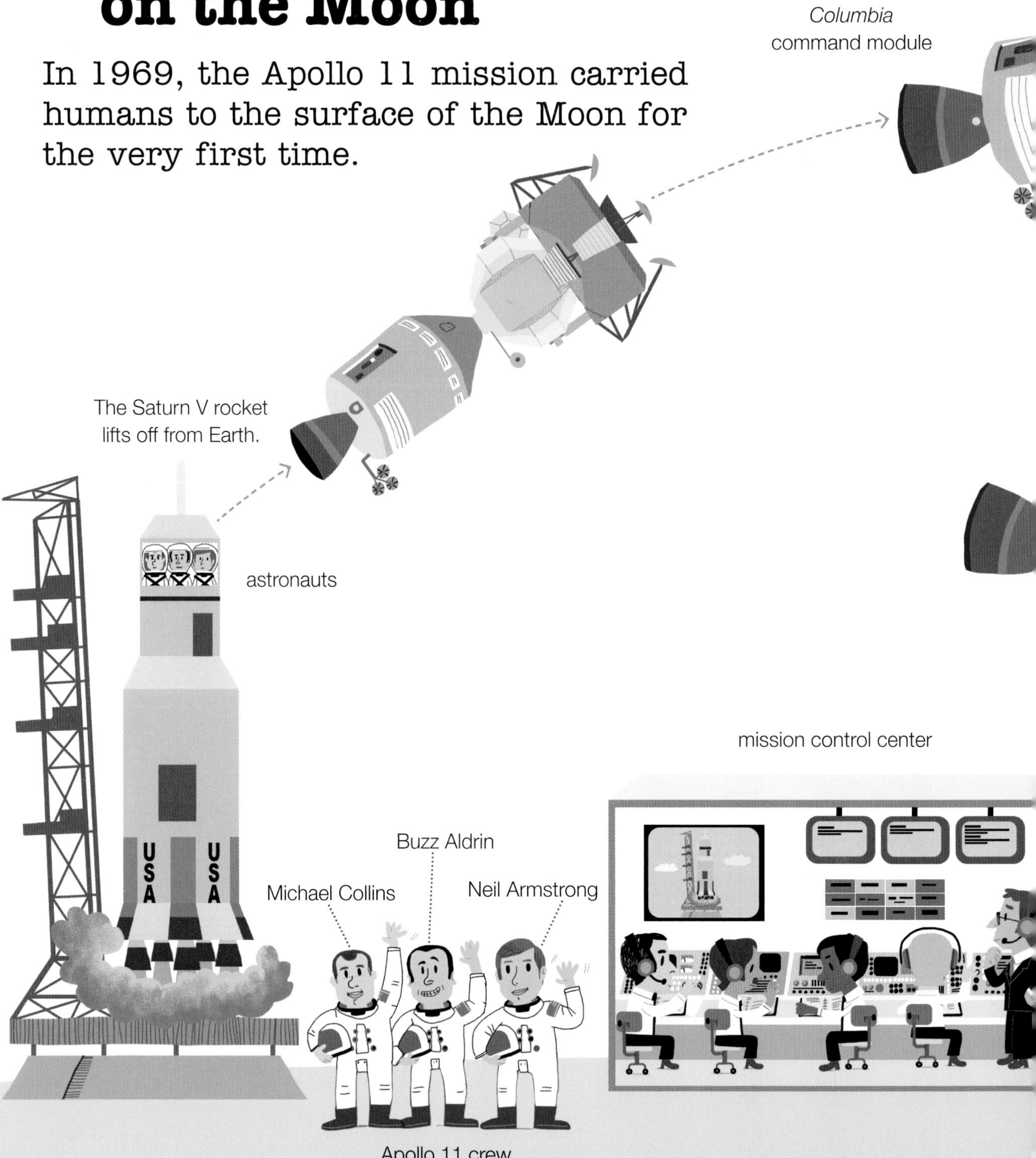

Columbia command module

The Saturn V rocket lifts off from Earth.

astronauts

mission control center

Buzz Aldrin

Michael Collins

Neil Armstrong

Apollo 11 crew

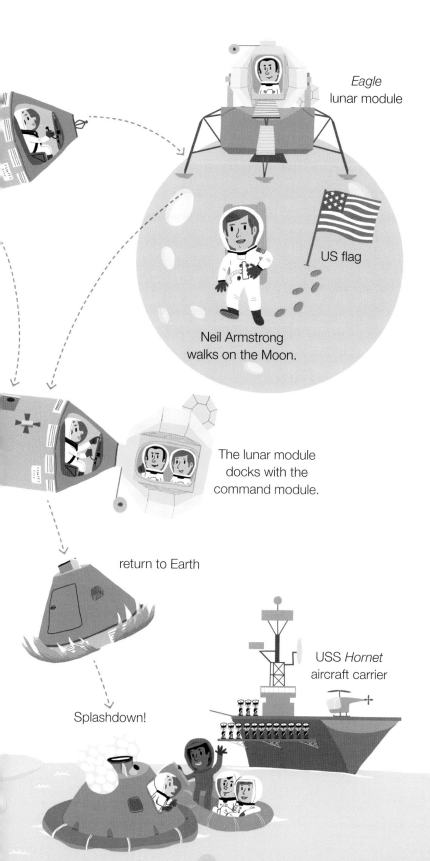

Eagle
lunar module

US flag

Neil Armstrong
walks on the Moon.

The lunar module
docks with the
command module.

return to Earth

USS *Hornet*
aircraft carrier

Splashdown!

Who
was the first space traveler

?

Neil Armstrong was the first person to walk on the Moon. But he wasn't the first person in space.

In 1961, Russian cosmonaut Yuri Gagarin became the first human in space. However, another traveler had already been there before him.

The very first space traveler was . . . a dog! Her name was Laika.

The Moon **29**
From Past to Present **56**

The International Space Station

The International Space Station (ISS) is a gigantic space laboratory where astronauts from all over the world conduct research and scientific experiments.

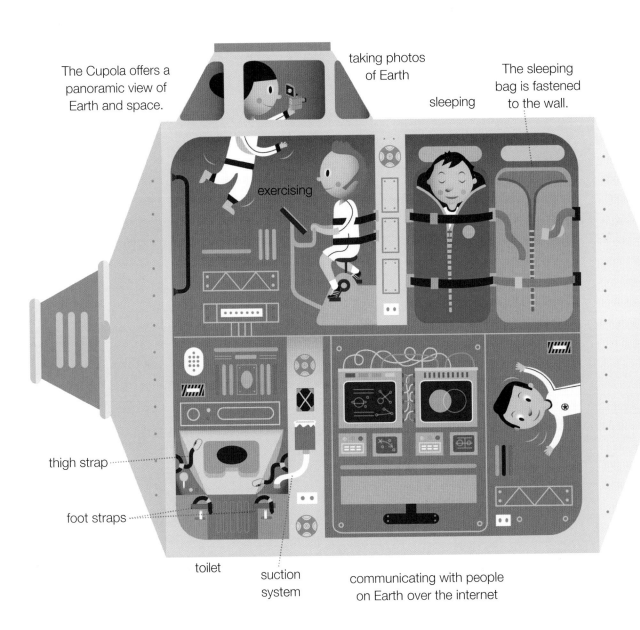

The Cupola offers a panoramic view of Earth and space.

taking photos of Earth

The sleeping bag is fastened to the wall.

sleeping

exercising

thigh strap

foot straps

toilet

suction system

communicating with people on Earth over the internet

growing
plants

conducting
experiments

hatch door   spacesuit

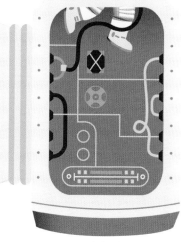

air lock

The ISS travels at 17,500 miles
(28,000 kilometers) per hour.

How
do astronauts
eat in space

?

When a spacecraft orbits Earth,
the motion makes people and
objects inside it weightless.

Astronauts don't drink from
cups, because their drinks
would float right out! Instead,
they drink from tightly sealed
pouches.

Most food is freeze-dried and
heated in an oven. Astronauts
have to fasten their food
containers to a tray, which is
attached to a wall or to their laps.

Resupplying the Space Station **66**
Going on a Spacewalk **68**

🛢 Resupplying the Space Station

Every two months, a spacecraft brings a fresh supply of water, food, equipment, and oxygen to the astronauts on the space station.

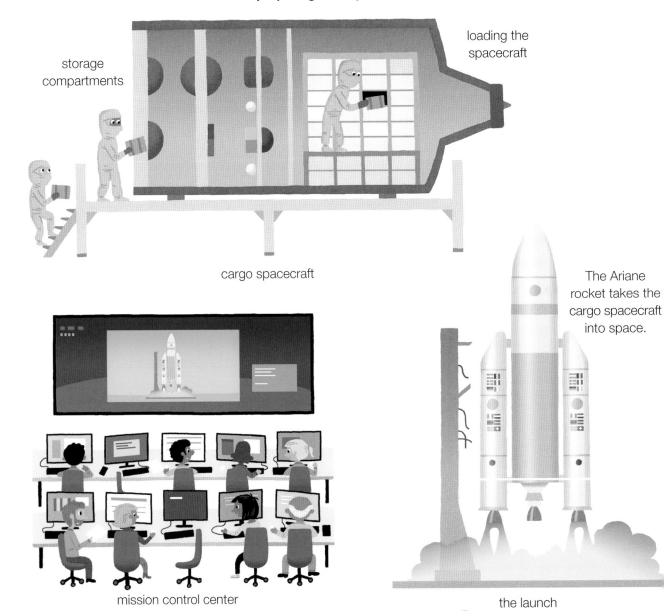

preparing for departure

storage compartments

loading the spacecraft

cargo spacecraft

The Ariane rocket takes the cargo spacecraft into space.

mission control center

the launch

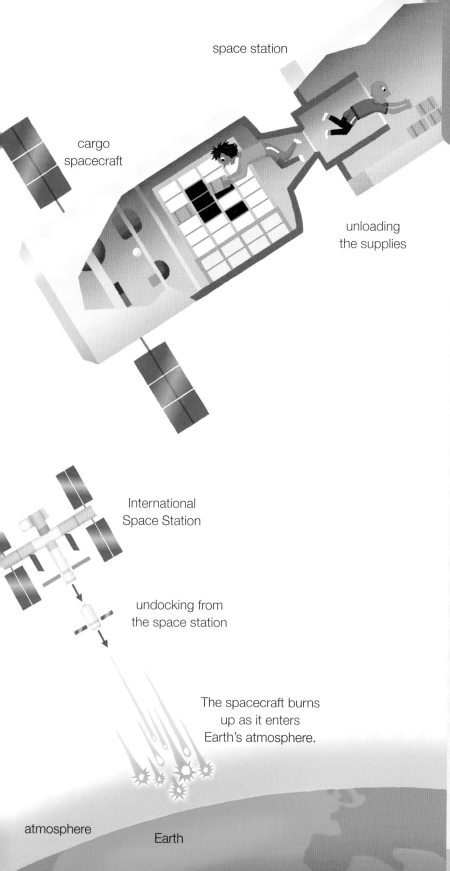

space station

cargo
spacecraft

unloading
the supplies

International
Space Station

undocking from
the space station

The spacecraft burns
up as it enters
Earth's atmosphere.

atmosphere   Earth

Using the toilet in space isn't
easy. Astronauts have to strap
themselves in to keep from
floating away.

An air jet sucks up the
astronauts' poop. It's stored with
other garbage.

The astronauts pee into a tube.
The urine is recycled and filtered
to produce drinking water.

Going on a Spacewalk

Astronauts often go on spacewalks to make repairs to the space station. They have to be well equipped while outside the station.

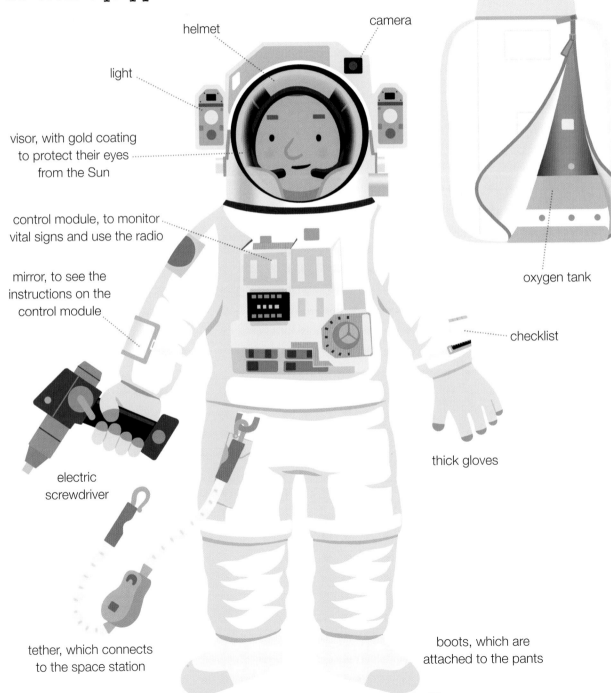

backpack with life-support system

helmet

camera

light

visor, with gold coating to protect their eyes from the Sun

control module, to monitor vital signs and use the radio

mirror, to see the instructions on the control module

oxygen tank

checklist

thick gloves

electric screwdriver

tether, which connects to the space station

boots, which are attached to the pants

clothing under
the spacesuit

cap

headphones

microphone

cooling system,
to keep from being too
hot in space

diaper, for relieving
themselves outside
the station

In addition to spacesuits,
astronauts wear a large pack
on their backs.

These backpacks contain
oxygen tanks, which supply
the astronauts with oxygen for
breathing while they're on a
spacewalk.

The astronauts also carry and
use tools that are easy to handle
while wearing bulky gloves.

Return to Earth

After staying on the space station for several months, the astronauts return to Earth aboard a Soyuz spacecraft.

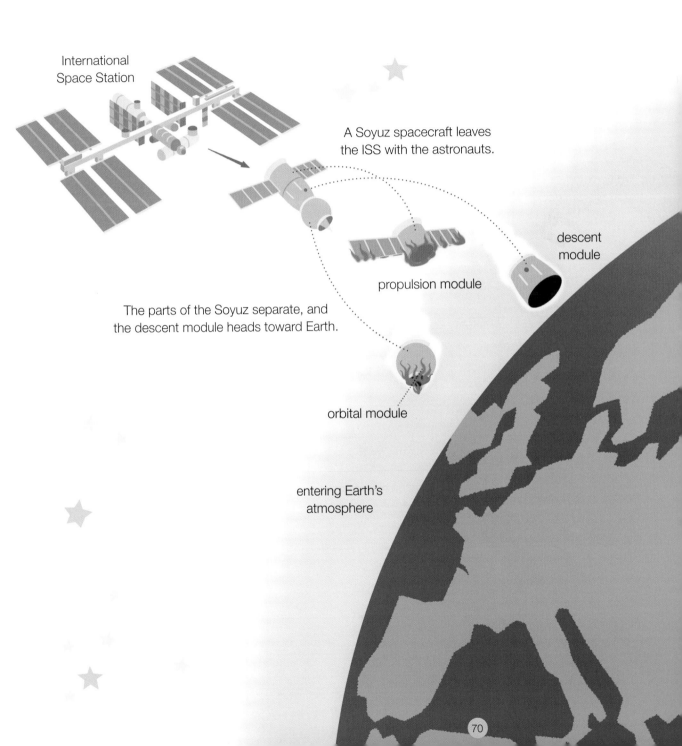

International Space Station

A Soyuz spacecraft leaves the ISS with the astronauts.

descent module

propulsion module

The parts of the Soyuz separate, and the descent module heads toward Earth.

orbital module

entering Earth's atmosphere

stars

atmosphere

Earth

parachute

The module slows down as it descends, thanks to parachutes and retro-rockets.

exhaust plume

landing

The hatch door opens.

news crew

How

long does it take to travel to and from the ISS ?

The trip to the ISS usually takes about six hours, but it could take longer. It depends on how quickly the spacecraft can catch up to the fast-moving space station.

However, the trip back is much faster: The journey lasts only three and a half hours.

After weeks of floating on the ISS, the astronauts have trouble standing up and need some help to leave the module. But their bodies quickly readjust.

High above Earth 46

The Flight 49

Future Space Travel

Scientists and inventors spend a lot of time planning for future expeditions to space—for research, vacations, or even a possible new home.

satellite

restaurant

mobile house

inventor

shuttle

astronaut

possible space station

garage

greenhouse

fitness center

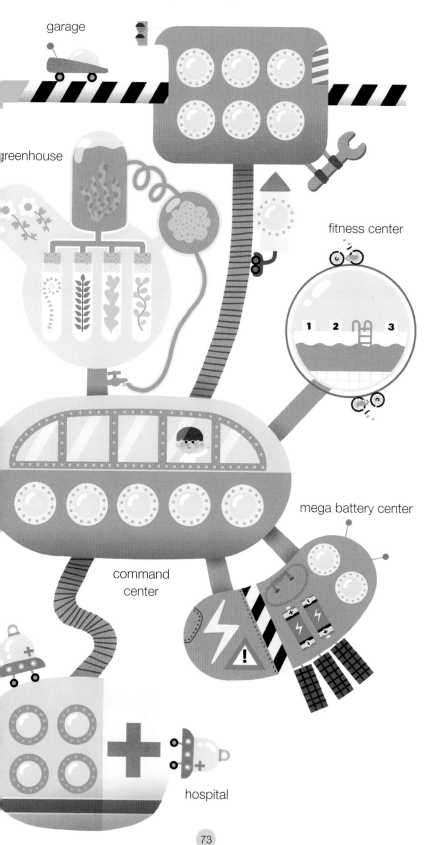

1 2 3

mega battery center

command center

hospital

At its closest point to Earth, Mars is 34 million miles (55 million kilometers) away.

It would take at least six months to get there, and just as long to get back.

CALENDAR

As we learn more about space and more advancements are made in technology, it might not be long before humans can travel to Mars.

Describe what is happening in this scene.

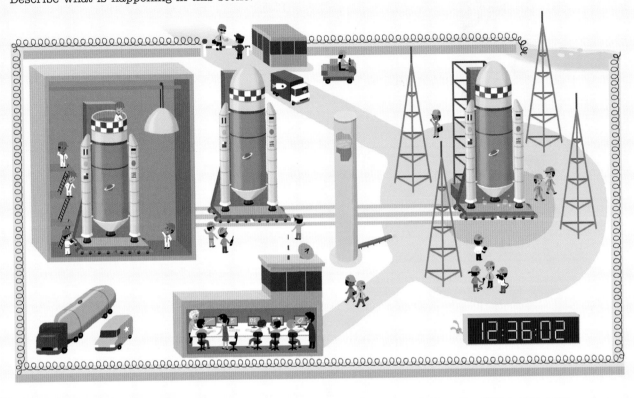

What do Michael Collins, Buzz Aldrin, and Neil Armstrong have in common?

Spot five differences between these two pictures.

 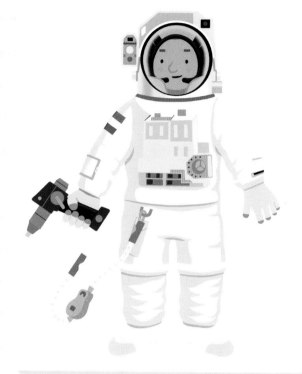

Astronauts undergo a lot of training
as they prepare for their space missions.
How do these activities help them?

Going to the bathroom in space takes extra equipment.
Which of these would you need to use a space toilet?

The astronauts have just landed back on Earth.
What do you think will happen next?

Index